Nettie's
GARDEN

Author: Heather Rae Weseman
Illustrator: Monique Turchan

Halo
Publishing International

ISBN 13: 978-1-61244-529-8
Library of Congress Control Number: 2017902451

Printed in the United States of America

Halo
Publishing International
www.halopublishing.com

Published by Halo Publishing International
1100 NW Loop 410
Suite 700 - 176
San Antonio, Texas 78213
Toll Free 1-877-705-9647
www.halopublishing.com
e-mail: contact@halopublishing.com

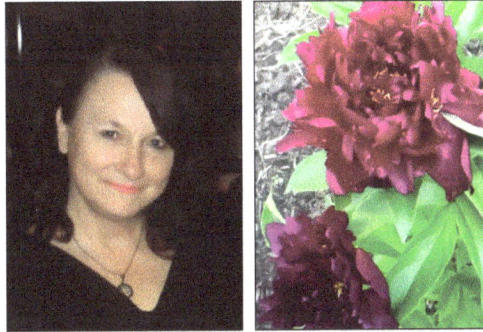

This story is in memory of my amazing mother, Jeannette. Every day
I am more thankful for your sacrificing love and example of being a godly
woman. Thank you for always pointing me to Jesus.
Can't wait until the moment we meet again.

Thank you to my Jesus for giving my family this story as an example of
your unending faithfulness. May all glory go to you! I pray that this will
touch the broken hearts of others and bring hope and healing.

My green stem was just starting to pop up out of the dark ground. The first glimpse of light was blinding it was so bright. As I adjusted to my surroundings, I saw a beautiful place with green plants of all different shapes and sizes. I also had a perfect view of the front window of the big, brown house where the family lived. They glanced out often to look at the birds, the other plants, and me.

Nettie, as the family called her, began to take care of me. She watered me, fed me, and kept the scary plants away from me. She often brought her radio with her and had beautiful music going. She would sing along with contentment on her face. Her children and dog would scamper about the yard, playing happily.

I was so excited to bloom and waited in anticipation each day. All the other plants were popping out in color every day. I couldn't wait to have Nettie see me in full bloom. As spring turned into summer, I noticed she often had a concerned look on her face as she tended to me, but she continued to care for me just as carefully as all the other plants in her garden.

And we know that in all things God works for the good of those who love him, who have been called according to his purpose.

Romans 8:28

Summer turned into fall, and fall turned into winter. I continued to enjoy watching the family. As the weather grew colder, the family stayed cozy and warm inside their house. They gathered around the woodstove and ate popcorn almost every evening. Even when the cold winter winds bitterly blew against the window, they laughed together and seemed unaware. My favorite was watching Nettie teach her children school lessons and about her Jesus. The children's faces of concentration, frustration, and joy at learning were entertaining.

Years went by, and I continued to grow, but I never bloomed. The other plants would look at me with dismay. Proudly, they would show their beautiful, bright colors. The thing that made me sad was disappointing Nettie. I remember once she said to me, "Don't worry. Your time will come," as she pulled a stubborn weed away from me. She was not giving up on me.

I also noticed Nettie slowing down. All her children eventually got married and moved away. Nettie didn't spend as much time with us in the garden as usual. She would gaze out her window in sadness. I knew she wanted to be with us, but she couldn't. Our home started to look neglected, and weeds were everywhere.

One happy day, her daughter and five little girls came. They started pulling all the weeds and giving us a drink of water. Soon our home looked beautiful! I noticed Nettie often looking out her window with a big smile on her face.

A few days later, early in the morning, I saw a bright light coming from the window. It was like nothing I had ever seen before.

Not long after that, Nettie's family and many other people came to the house. There were tears and much sadness in the home. Nettie was gone.

Then it was her husband who would just stare sadly out the window. But something strange was happening to me. I could feel it in my roots. Another day began, and I saw Nettie's husband sadly gazing out the window, wiping away tears. Something dark pink in color caught my eye, and he saw it, too. He had a look of surprise on his face. He was soon outside, kneeling down beside me. I felt water on my leaves. It was his tears.

After twenty-five years, I had bloomed. Beautiful maroon petals stuck to me. I remembered Nettie telling me that my time would come. I now know why God had me wait all those years for this very moment. The whole family happily came to see me. They took pictures, and I could see a look of hope from them for the first time since Nettie's disappearance from this earth. God showed them hope in my colors, that life can still be new and good. Just as I had bloomed, I knew Nettie was also in full bloom in heaven with her Jesus.

Every year, I continue to have more and more flowers poking out of me. The family always comes and smells my sweet scent and acts like I am the most beautiful flower they have ever seen. I remind them of hope in a very dark time. Though it was hard to be patient, I am so glad that God had me wait for a time such as this! God can turn ordinary things into miraculous events. I am just a simple peony plant, but God made me special in His own time.

www.ingramcontent.com/pod-product-compliance
Lightning Source LLC
LaVergne TN
LVHW070839080426
835511LV00025B/3483